Home Organizing Guru
Establishing a Successful Professional Organizing Business

Table of Contents

Chapter 1. Introduction

Welcome to an enlightening journey that seeks to elevate your personal potential into a booming business! Our Special Report entitled "Home Organizing Guru: Establishing a Successful Professional Organizing Business" is your ticket to transforming clutter into clarity, disorganization into order, and chaos into calm. Sprinkled with magic dust of practical wisdom, insider secrets, and engaging anecdotes, this report is a must-have for anyone with a knack for neatness, a passion for helping others bring order into their lives, and a vision to turn this passion into a profitable venture. Intriguing, uplifting, and laden with actionable insights, allow this Special Report to be your guiding light as you embark on the exciting journey of becoming a successful Home Organizing Guru.

Chapter 2. Unleashing the Organizer Within

You may not believe it, but within you lies the capacity to become a highly effective and successful home organizer. The first step in realizing this potential is recognizing your inherent organizing abilities and nurturing them.

2.1. Discovering your Organizing Abilities

The journey to being a successful home organizer starts with self-awareness. Each one of us possesses a range of skills that, when identified and honed, can be invaluable in organizing. These skills can include problem-solving, creativity, time management, or even something as simple as paying attention to details.

To identify these skills, you can do a simple exercise. Make a list of tasks you do effortlessly, areas where people often compliment you or situations where you feel the most satisfaction. Once you identify these skills, prop yourself to refine them further and become a master in utilising them effectively for home organization.

2.2. The Art of Visualization

Visualization is an essential skill for organizing. It allows you to envision the potential of space, helping you devise ingenious ways of making the most out of it. Start by practicing visualization with a simple exercise: Choose a small area in your home that you believe can be better organized. Assess it critically and imagine the various ways you can improve it based on your needs, available space, and existing materials. Work on transforming that space according to your visualization. Remember, practice makes perfect!

2.3. Problem-Solving Skills

A successful organizer possesses excellent problem-solving skills. Every organizing project will present its unique challenges that require innovative solutions. Whether it is figuring out how to maximize a small closet space or deciding the best way to organize a chaotic kitchen, your problem-solving skills will be your greatest allies.

One way to sharpen these skills is by taking on DIY projects. Such tasks push your creativity, resourcefulness, and problem-solving skills. Remember, an organizer's primary role is to create systems out of chaos, and problem-solving is at the heart of this mission.

2.4. Working with Different Personalities

To succeed as a home organizer, you have to work with people effectively. Every client is unique, with different needs and personalities. Some may be resistant to changes, while others may feel overwhelmed by the thought of letting go of things. Your job as an organizer will be to guide your clients gently through these emotional hurdles and help them embrace a more organized lifestyle.

Invest time in improving your people skills. Understanding different personality types and their characteristics can help you tailor your approach to match your client's specific needs and preferences.

2.5. Mastering Time Management

Time management is a critical skill for home organizers. It ensures you not only finish your projects on time but also create sustainable systems that your clients can maintain. By effectively managing your time, you devise ways to streamline the process, eliminating redundant steps and making the entire process efficient.

A recommended approach is to adopt a time management technique that suits your work style. Techniques like the Pomodoro Technique or the Eisenhower Matrix can be some great methods to begin your time management journey.

2.6. Fostering Adaptability

Being adaptable is another important trait of a successful home organizer. Since every home and every individual is unique, scenarios you encounter will often be different. What worked for one project may not be effective for another. Cultivate adaptability by constantly learning and trying new organizing methods and tools. Be open to changing your strategies based on the requirements of the project.

2.7. In the End, It's about Empathy

Finally, remember that your role as an organizer is not just about creating beautiful spaces; it's about bringing comfort, peace, and happiness into people's lives. Empathy and understanding are key to understanding your clients' unique challenges and providing solutions that truly impact their lives.

In the end, becoming a successful home organizer is a journey of self-discovery and growth. It's about honing the organizer within you and offering it as a service to others to help them lead a more decluttered, organized, and happier life. As you embark on this journey, remember that your passion, coupled with commitment and dedication, can transform you into a highly successful Home Organizing Guru.

Chapter 3. Blueprint to a Thriving Organizing Business

Success in the professional organizing business rarely happens by accident. It involves careful planning, strategic decision-making, and constant evolution. Embracing this truth is your first step toward creating a thriving organizing business. In this comprehensive chapter, we will unfold a blueprint that will provide keen insights into starting and successfully running an organizing business.

3.1. Establishing Your Business

Coming up with a business plan lays the groundwork for your business' future and sets a concrete path for it to follow. This plan should include your business' mission statement, a SWOT analysis (Strengths, Weaknesses, Opportunities, Threats), and projections for growth. Make sure to spend adequate time crafting this pivotal document, as it will be your reference point when making major business decisions.

Next, you'll need to choose your business name carefully. The name should be concise, meaningful, and reflective of the services you provide. Remember, your business name should resonate with potential clients and paint a vivid image of what you offer.

Officially register and set up your business accordingly, considering various elements such as location, tax requirements, permits, and licensing. You can opt for a home-based business for starters or rent a space based on your budget and strategic needs.

3.2. Specializing and Pricing

Deciding on your specialization is key to differentiating your business in the market. Explore specializations like residential organizing, workplace organizing, downsizing seniors, relocating services, or event planning. Your expertise and interests should guide you on what segment will work best for you.

After defining your specialization, you need to construct an intuitive pricing structure. Bring in the elements of time, effort, project complexity, and market standards while deciding your charges. It is essential to communicate your fees transparently and confidently to your clients.

3.3. Building a Robust Online Presence

In our digital age, having a professional website and an active social media presence is no longer a luxury but a necessity. Ensure your website is user-friendly, eye-catching, accessible and provides potential clients with all the necessary information about your services.

Harness the power of social media platforms like Facebook, Instagram, Pinterest, and Twitter by frequently sharing helpful tips, success stories, testimonials, and interesting organizing hacks. Social media strategy is potent for creating brand awareness and credibility.

3.4. Networking and Collaboration

Join local, national, or international professional organizing associations to gain from their vast resources, seminars, and training programs. Networking with other professionals in your field can lead to invaluable insights, partnerships, and collaborations, significantly benefitting your organizational growth.

3.5. Building a Clientele & Retention

Obtain new clients by word-of-mouth, references, client testimonials, advertising, or offering introductory discounts. After winning clients, implement stringent procedures to exceed their expectations. Outstanding client satisfaction can guarantee recurring business.

Strive to build long-term relationships with your clients by regular follow-ups, giving them tips for maintaining the organization, and going beyond their expectations.

3.6. Scaling Your Business

As your organizing business grows, consider expanding your services, hiring employees, and even franchising. Ensure you have robust systems and processes in place before scaling up.

3.7. Professional Development

Never stop honing your skills and evolving your techniques. Continue to learn about industry trends and attend professional development courses. Staying up-to-date and adaptable is crucial in an ever-changing market.

3.8. The Importance of Self-Care

Don't ignore the importance of self-care. Running a business can often become stressful; prioritizing your well-being is not only beneficial for you but also impacts your business positively.

Ultimately, your professional organizing business's success depends on your passion, commitment, and unwavering desire to help others. By following the blueprint highlighted in this chapter, you are well on your way to establishing a thriving and fulfilling professional organizing business.

Chapter 4. Home Organizing Basics: A Comprehensive Guide

Whether just getting started in the world of home organizing or enhancing your professional craft, understanding the nuts and bolts of organizing is nothing short of essential. Successful home organizers are adept at mastering these basics and using them to transform spaces into functional and aesthetic surroundings that both comfort and inspire their clients.

4.1. The Core Principles of Organizing

The fundamentals of home organizing come down to understanding and applying a few key principles. These include sorting, categorizing, decluttering, and systemizing items. Expecting to magically create order out of chaos without these principles would be like attempting to build a house without a blueprint.

1. Sorting: The initial step in organizing any space involves sorting items into like groups. By grouping similar items together, it makes it easier to assess what a client has and what they need.

> Example:
> In a kitchen, you might sort items into categories such as cookware, utensils, baking supplies, packaged foods, fresh produce, and so on.

1. Categorizing: After the sorting process, the next step involves categorizing the sorted items. This can be based on their purpose,

frequency of use, or any other client-specific criteria.

> Example:
> In an office, you might categorize items based on job
> function: paperwork, office supplies, technology, books,
> etc.

1. Decluttering: This process involves helping a client decide what items to keep, discard, donate, or sell. It can be a challenging step for many, as it often involves emotional decisions.

> Example:
> In a bedroom, you may help the client declutter by
> asking questions such as, "When was the last time you
> wore this?" or, "Does this item bring you joy or serve a
> practical purpose?"

1. Systemizing: This final step involves creating a logical and manageable system that the client can maintain long term. This often requires establishing zones and implementing storage solutions.

> Example:
> In a craft room, you may create a system where all
> painting supplies are stored together, all sewing items
> in another zone, and paper crafts in another, and so on.

4.2. The Importance of a Customized Approach

Universal organizing strategies can provide a framework, but the success of your organizing services largely hinges on delivering personalized solutions that resonate with individual client needs and lifestyles. This requires acute observation, listening skills, and empathy.

A customized approach appreciates every client's unique style, habits, culture, and values. It means taking into account the client's tastes, budget, the physical layout of their space, their organizational challenges, and desired outcomes. The goal is to create structure and systems that are instinctive, natural, and easy to maintain, thus enhancing the client's quality of life.

4.3. The Essential Tools of the Trade

While mastering organizing techniques and developing great client relationships are crucial, having the right tools for the job plays a significant role in your success. Here are a few essentials:

1. Measuring Tape: A measuring tape is indispensable when evaluating spaces and choosing the right storage solutions.

2. Labels and Label Maker: Clearly marked boxes, bins, and drawers make maintaining order much easier for clients.

3. Storage Materials: All types of bins, baskets, shelves, and hooks come in handy when creating effective storage solutions.

4. Cleaning Supplies: A clean space is as important as an organized one. Always have basic cleaning products and tools on hand.

4.4. Space Planning and Storage Solutions

One of the key skills of a proficient home organizer is the ability to create effective space plans that maximize both functionality and aesthetics. It involves being able to envision the space's potential, seeing beyond the clutter, and creating orderly zones that serve specific purposes.

Equally vital is the selection and implementation of accessible, visually pleasing storage solutions that complement the client's style and preferences. When choosing and setting up storage solutions, practicality, durability, and scalability should be considered.

4.5. Effective Client Communication

Being an excellent communicator, listener, and negotiator forms a significant part of a home organizer's job. Clients may resist changes or have emotional reactions during the decluttering process. Guiding them through these moments with empathy, patience, and diplomacy is important.

4.6. Planning Your Home Organizing Sessions

Planning your sessions enables you to be efficient and deliver visible results without overwhelming your client. For maximum efficiency, you may choose to focus on one area per session, starting from the most cluttered or bothering area.

4.7. Outcome Evaluation

Regular outcome evaluation is crucial in ensuring your solutions are functional and maintained. It includes checking in with your client after a week or a month to see how they're adjusting to new systems, what's working, and what may need improvements.

In conclusion, understanding and implementing these home organizing basics are your first steps in serving your clients effectively and transforming your passion into a thriving business. As you foster these skills and apply them, you are on your way to becoming a truly transformative Home Organizing Guru.

Chapter 5. Niche Expertise: Cultivating Your Unique Style

The journey of becoming a successful Home Organizing Guru begins with understanding your unique aptitudes and strengths. This is where cultivating your niche expertise comes into play. Achieving a unique style is no accident, but a deliberate, conscious, and continuously refined process.

5.1. Identifying Your Strengths

Becoming aware of your strengths is the first step towards cultivating a unique style. What are you most passionate about within the realm of home organization? Is there a specific area where you consistently excel, perhaps organizing small spaces, children's rooms, or home offices? Take time to introspect and identify these areas.

Don't hesitate to solicit feedback from family, friends, or anyone who has experienced your work. Their insights can often bubble up strengths you've been too humble to notice, or areas you enjoy but didn't think were significant.

5.2. Nurturing Your Passion

Imbuing your work with passion isn't an option, but a necessity. Passion is infectious; your clients will feel, value and respect it. By nurturing your passion for your favored area, you start to develop a unique style. Speak, read, learn, and involve yourself in your chosen niche as much as possible.

5.3. Learning Continually

Even with identified strengths and passion, you need to continuously learn. As American Journalist Gene Fowler wisely said, "Writing is easy. All you do is stare at a blank sheet of paper until drops of blood form on your forehead". Mastery requires patience, practice, and continual learning—embrace them all.

Continuously update your knowledge by reading books, attending workshops, and networking with fellow professionals. Don't shy away from challenges—they're chances to learn. Remember, each knowledge nugget you acquire and experience you gain brings you one step closer to expert.

5.4. Adopting a Client-Focused Approach

Understanding your client's needs and personal style is crucial. After all, home organization isn't solely about tidiness, it's a means of enhancing your client's lifestyle.

Every client comes with unique needs, habits, preferences, and lifestyles. Dive deep and understand these aspects before you begin organizing. Develop an empathetic approach; understanding the underlying reasons for clutter can provide insights into solutions that will truly work for your client.

5.5. Developing Your Methods

In time, you will start seeing patterns in your approach to different projects. This is your unique methodology developing. Pay attention to these patterns and refine them. It will help your style become more recognizable and also improve your efficiency.

Whether you're a fan of the KonMari method, prefer a more minimalist approach, or love color-coded systems, your methodology forms the backbone of your unique style as a home organization professional.

5.6. Crafting Your Narrative

The way that you communicate with your clients and market your services plays a significant role in establishing your unique style. So purposely craft your narrative. The most successful professionals have a consistent and engaging way of presenting themselves and their work.

Whether it's through before-and-after photos, client testimonials, or social media, every piece of communication from your end should reflect your unique style and niche expertise.

5.7. Collaborating and Networking

Don't underestimate the power of networking. By engaging with other professionals in your field, you can gain fresh insights and perspectives. Collaborating with other professionals can also provide opportunities to work on pioneering projects that can shape your unique style even further.

5.8. Embracing Feedback

Embrace all feedback constructively. Understand that both positive and negative feedback provide opportunities to learn and grow. Positive feedback reaffirms you're on the right path, while constructive criticism shows you where you can improve.

5.9. Never Compromising on Quality

Last but by no means least, consistently high-quality work is an essential part of cultivating your unique style. Remember, your work directly impacts your client's lives, and they trust you to deliver organizational solutions that make their lives better.

In conclusion, cultivating your niche expertise and unique style is far from an overnight process, it's an exciting journey. Identify your strengths, nurture your passion, learn continually, adopt a client-focused approach, develop your methods, craft your narrative, embrace feedback, collaborate and network with others, but most importantly, never compromise on the quality of your work. Your commitment to these steps will help you to develop a distinctive and valued style, fortifying your position as a sought-after Home Organizing Guru.

Chapter 6. Building a Loyal Clientele: Secrets to Customer Satisfaction

Building a loyal customer base is central to the long-term success of any business, including your professional Home Organizing enterprise. This chapter will delve into strategies, secrets, anecdotes, and practical tips for maximizing customer satisfaction, systematic client engagement, and effective relationship management. The golden thread weaving through this entire discourse is the principle of delighting your clients beyond the standard business exchange, to foster enduring loyalty and thriving word-of-mouth endorsements.

6.1. Understanding your Clients

Personal home organizing is an intimately private service that calls for a keen understanding of your client's unique needs, preferences, and their inherent relationship with their living environment. It's not just about organizing physical spaces. Fundamentally, it's about understanding a client's lifestyle, their perspectives, personal habits, preferences and bringing calm to the storm's eye.

Client Interview – A thorough client interview will root out their specific needs and expectations. Ask open-ended questions about their lifestyle, organizing challenges, what an ideal organized space looks like for them, and how they envision maintaining it.

Space Evaluation – Inspect the space in need of organization. Always remember to ask for permission as this is a personal space you are entering. Space evaluation will give you insights into the client's habits and help tailor your organizing strategy.

Personalized Recommendations – Equipped with the gathered information, provide tailor-made organizing solutions. Explain the recommendations, the reasons behind each suggestion, and the benefits the client will gain.

6.2. Exceeding Expectations

When you proceed to organize, ensure you perform beyond expectations. Clients value unexpected extra touches, surprises, or perks only if they are relevant and highly personalized.

Quality of Service – Consistently delivering high-quality service trumps all other customer satisfaction strategies. This includes timeliness, professionalism, courteous behavior, and attention to detail.

Customized Organizing Methods – Do not stick with a one-size-fits-all approach. Recognize that each client is unique and customize your organizing techniques to match their preferences.

After-Service Follow-ups – Once the job is done, don't just walk away. Contact your clients after a couple of weeks to see how the new organization system is working out for them. You might provide tips and solutions for any new challenges they may face.

6.3. Building Long-Term Relationships

Beyond the initial project, aim to cultivate long-term relationships with your clients. Regularly keep in touch without being intrusive.

Periodic Check-ins – Reach out every few months to see how they're maintaining the space. They might require some tweaking or even a new project.

Special Occasions – Send a card during holiday seasons or birthdays.

It's a simple gesture that maintains a connection and shows that you care.

Referral Discounts – Offer small discounts or perks for every successful referral. It's a win-win situation that benefits both parties while reinforcing a positive client relationship.

6.4. Handling Criticism and Failures

There may come a time when clients are not wholly satisfied with your service. The key is not to react defensively but to use it as a stepping stone to improve.

Accept and Apologize – If you've made a mistake, own up to it and apologize. The client will appreciate your honesty.

Ask for Feedback – Encourage clients to provide constructive feedback and suggestions. Show gratitude for their input and treat it as valuable information to improve your services.

Make Amends – Whenever possible and reasonable, offer to correct the issues or provide discounts on future services.

6.5. Harnessing Testimonials and Referrals

Satisfied clients are your greatest marketing agents. At the end of a successful job, politely ask them to provide testimonials or refer your service to their friends and family.

Request for Testimonials – An affirmation of quality service from a delighted client can be used on your website, marketing materials, and social media channels. Always ask for permission before you share their testimonial.

Encourage Referrals – Suggest clients to spread the word about your services. Remind them about your referral program if one exists.

Customer satisfaction entails much more than providing an excellent service. It's about building connections, exceeding expectations, handling criticism, and maximizing the power of satisfied clients. Cultivate a harmonious balance of these elements to build a loyal customer base that takes your professional home organizing business to greater heights. Bear in mind that the best businesses grow through satisfied customers who become ambassadors of their exceptional experience.

Chapter 7. Marketing Magic for the Modern Organizer

Before we plunge into the multifaceted world of marketing, it's essential to grasp one key principle: marketing is not about selling, it's about creating need and fostering relationships. It's about connecting with your clients in meaningful ways and proving that your services can make a tangible difference in their lives. Now, let's delve into the practicalities of marketing for the modern day Home Organizer.

7.1. Know Your Value Proposition

Given the competitive market landscape, it's critical to distinguish your business from others. Your value proposition is what differentiates you - it's the reason why people would consider your service over others. Outline the unique benefits you offer and what makes your service special. Remember, your value proposition should resonate with your clients and address their needs, their pain points, and the issues they care about.

7.2. Define Your Target Audience

The next crucial step is understanding your target audience. Are they busy working professionals who need help organizing their home offices? Or perhaps they are parents struggling to manage their children's toys and study areas? Defining your ideal clients helps you tailor your offerings and effectively address their specific needs.

Creating buyer personas could be helpful. A buyer persona is a fictional characterization of your ideal customer based on your market research and data about your existing customers. Include details like age, household size, occupation, income, and key challenges. This helps create content and marketing messages that appeal directly to them.

7.3. Build a Strong Online Presence

In the digital age, having a well-optimized, professional website that mirrors your brand's essence and value proposition is vital. An engaging and easy-to-navigate website is a powerful marketing tool. It enables prospective clients to find you online, learn about your services, and makes it simple for them to get in touch.

Social media platforms like Instagram, Facebook, and Pinterest are great places to showcase your work, engage with your potential clients, and convey your unique approach to home organization. These digital platforms offer excellent opportunities for pictures and videos - visual proof of the transformative impact your services can offer.

Don't forget about SEO (Search Engine Optimization). Make sure your website and online content are optimized with keywords related to home organizing to boost your visibility in search engine results.

7.4. Content Marketing and Blogging

Provide valuable content to your current and potential clients. This could be in the form of blog posts, eBooks, newsletters, or how-to videos. Not only does this position you as an expert in your field, but it also helps build trust with your audience. Make sure to promote your content across your social media platforms, website, and email marketing campaigns.

7.5. Networking and Community

Networking with related businesses like real estate agents, interior designers, or home improvement stores can provide referrals and open up spaces for collaboration. Be active in community events and consider donating your services to charitable causes or events to raise your business profile.

7.6. Testimonials and Word-of-Mouth Marketing

Happy clients are your best advocates. Encourage them to leave testimonials and share their positive experiences with friends and family. Word-of-mouth marketing can be incredibly powerful and can help legitimize your services in the eyes of potential clients.

7.7. Paid Advertising and Promotions

Consider investing in targeted local advertising and promotions, whether that's in print media or online. Boosting social media posts or running Google Ad campaigns can be effective tactics for reaching potential clients in your area. Offering promotions or discounts for first-time clients can also help draw in business.

Remember, effective marketing takes time; it's about continuous learning and adapting to evolving market trends and client needs. The exciting part of being a Home Organizing Guru is that you are in a dynamic, people-driven business that allows you to continuously evolve, affect meaningful change, and see tangible results of your work. With this comprehensive marketing guide, you're well-equipped to create a memorable brand that resonates with your clients, drives demand for your services, and propels your business to new heights.

Chapter 8. Leveraging Social Media for Your Business

In the digital age, mastery of social media is not merely an afterthought, but a vital ingredient for the success recipe of your professional organizing business. Social media platforms present a plethora of opportunities to connect with your audience, savvy marketing, as well as a platform to display the marvels of your organizing prowess. Harnessing this power can transform your humble venture into a noteworthy brand.

8.1. Understanding Your Platforms

There are numerous social media platforms that can be leveraged to expand your business. However, not all platforms are created equal. Each platform has its unique prospects best suited to reach certain demographics or types of content.

Facebook: With over 2.7 billion monthly active users, Facebook is a broadcasting powerhouse. This platform is particularly beneficial for reaching older demographics, as about 70% of adults aged 50 to 64 use Facebook.

Instagram: Aesthetics are at the core of Instagram, making it a perfect platform for a professional organiser. Over a billion people use Instagram monthly, and it skews younger, with the largest demographic being people aged 25 to 34.

Pinterest: Ideal for DIY and creative content, Pinterest allows you to create 'pins' reflecting your work. It's highly visual and has a predominantly female user base, making it an ideal platform for home organization ideas.

LinkedIn: A professional networking platform where businesses and professionals connect, excellent for B2B prospects.

Twitter: Allows you to broadcast brief messages to your followers. Best suited for sharing news, updates, and engaging in the current popular discourse.

8.2. Creating Engaging Content

Social media algorithms are discerning and favor engaging content. Rather than solely sharing promotional content, strike a balance with content that educates, inspires, and prompts conversation.

Showcase Transformations: Before and after images are excellent ways to illustrate your skills. However, consider leveling up this classic post type by explaining the process behind the transformation. What specific organizing principles did you apply? What challenges did you face, and how did you overcome them?

Educational Posts: Create content that educates your audience on organizing principles. Infographics, blog posts, and videos are some formats you can use. Break down complex methods into comprehensible bits. Remember, the ultimate goal is to evoke a sense of "I can do this too!".

Behind-the-scenes: A glimpse behind the scenes humanizes your brand. Show them the work behind those pristine pictures: the sweat, the occasional chaos, and yes, even the contained disarray that comes before a significant transformation.

8.3. Building A Community

Social media platforms offer potential to cultivate meaningful communities around your brand. Followers can become an engaged community when they feel involved in the brand's journey.

Interactive Contents: Encourage participation with regular Q&As,

feedback requests, quizzes, contests, and more. Make your followers feel valued by involving them in your decisions.

Highlight Customer Stories: Shine some light on your clients. If they're comfortable with it, share their organising journeys – from the initial challenges, through the process, to the final results. Authentic stories can be profoundly impactful.

Engagement Groups: Depending on the platform, participate in or create engagement groups. These groups create a virtuous cycle of engagement that can help each member account increase visibility.

8.4. Consistency is Key

Frequent and consistent posting is crucial for online presence. It keeps your brand at the forefront of your followers' minds and helps improve your algorithmic ranking.

Create a content calendar to ensure regular posting. Make sure to include a blend of different post types and keep track of what content performs best.

8.5. Leveraging Social Media Tools

There are numerous tools designed to help manage your social media efforts.

Scheduling Tools: Tools like Hootsuite, Buffer, or Later allow you to schedule posts across platforms, making consistency much easier to achieve.

Analytics Tools: Understanding your performance is critical. Many platforms have built-in analytics, but tools like Sprout Social offer more in-depth insights.

Graphic Design Tools: Canva, Adobe Spark Post, and others can help you create professional-looking graphics without needing a design background.

In conclusion, social media is a double-edged sword. It's fraught with challenges, yet holds immense possibilities. By understanding your platforms, creating engaging content, fostering a community, posting consistently, and making good use of social media management tools, you can transform ordinary social media platforms into a power-packed arsenal for your business's growth and success. The world is but a click away; embrace the adventure of social media, and watch your professional organizing business flourish.

Chapter 9. Navigating Financials: Pricing and Billing Decoded

The process of establishing your professional organizing business requires an in-depth study of financial planning and management. Two critical areas to understand deeply are your pricing strategy and billing system. Without a thorough grasp of these, even the most passionate organizers may find it challenging to maintain a profitable business.

9.1. Understanding Your Costs

Before setting your prices, you'll need to have a thorough understanding of your costs. Some initial costs include acquiring office space (if applicable), getting licensed, and purchasing supplies and equipment. However, overhead costs usually don't end after the business gets launched. Ongoing expenses include utilities and services such as internet connectivity, phone lines, software subscriptions, insurance, marketing and advertising expenses, and even your time.

To gain a realistic view of your financial necessities, start by noting down all your known costs. After that, set aside a financial cushion to cover unforeseen expenditures. Ensure that your business prices reflect these costs, so you don't end up running a deficit.

9.2. Setting Your Prices

When it comes to setting prices for your services, several factors come into play. These include the average market rate for home organizing services in your locality, the complexity and scope of each job, and the value you are providing to your clients. Provide a balance between competitive pricing and delivering a value-rich service. Underpricing your services may attract customers quickly, but it can also devalue your expertise, trap you in a cycle of overwork and underpayment, and potentially lead to financial losses.

On the other hand, overpricing your services can deter potential clients. The sweet spot is to find a pricing strategy that adequately compensates for your expertise and time without alienating customers. It's helpful to do some research on what other professional organizers in your area are charging for a better pricing perspective.

9.3. Developing a Billing System

Once your pricing strategy is in place, you'll need to develop an efficient billing system. The billing system you employ should be easy for you and your clients to navigate. It could be beneficial for you to outline your terms of payment in your contract or agreement. This way, your clients clearly understand when and how to make a payment, which can reduce any scope of misunderstandings and disputes later on.

The advancement of technology has led to an abundance of software options that can make this process simple and organized. Investing in a good billing and invoicing system can lead to smooth and seamless transactions, prompt payments, and even saves your valuable time.

9.4. Offering Payment Plans

Every client's financial situation differs, and recognizing this can give your business a competitive edge. Offering flexible payment plans can be a determining factor for clients choosing between your services and a competitor's.

Comprehend your client's perspective by addressing their needs. An upfront payment might work for some, but others may be more comfortable and appreciative of a weekly or monthly plan. Such a model keeps you and your client on the same page and can pave the way for a great professional relationship.

9.5. Delving into Discounts

While it's crucial to fully value your time and expertise, you might also consider offering discounts on certain occasions, for instance, as a first-time client offer or during a festive season. By integrating a strategic discount system, you can attract more customers, stimulate business during slower periods, and even encourage referrals. However, ensure that your discounted price still covers your costs and yields a profit.

9.6. Evaluating Your Financial Performance

Once your business starts rolling, it's advisable to periodically evaluate your financial performance. This entails tracking and analyzing your revenue, expenses, cash flow, and overall profitability. With regular financial assessments, you can quickly spot trends, fluctuations, and issues, make timely adjustments, and continuously improve your financial health.

Creating a successful home organizing business involves more than just a keen eye for order and a knack for transforming spaces. It requires a robust pricing and billing strategy that supports your financial needs, respects your talents and time, and meets your clients' expectations. By mastering the financial aspects of your business, you can ensure that your passion is not just fulfilling but also financially rewarding.

Chapter 10. Growth Strategies: Scaling Your Organizing Business

Every successful story of business growth consists of effective planning and strategic adaptation to market dynamics. In the world of professional organizing, one must understand, innovate, and execute plans that aim at the systematic expansion of the business, without compromising the quality of the services.

10.1. Scaling Through Building a Powerful Brand

Creating a distinct brand identity is the primary step towards scaling your business. The brand should reflect your philosophy and the uniqueness of your services. Use catchy and memorable slogans, logos, and taglines that will help clients remember your business.

Invest in a professionally designed logo and create a corresponding color scheme for your business. These are visual cues that help potential clients associate with your brand on different platforms.

Develop a clear and compelling brand message, one that resonates with your target audience. Make it evident how choosing your organizing services will bring a meaningful difference to their lives.

Consider your brand as a person. A brand personification means giving your brand characteristics like empathy or trustworthiness. This forms an emotional connection with your clients, encouraging their loyalty towards your brand.

10.2. Expanding Clientele Through Effective Marketing

Once your brand is in place, expose it to the right audience. For marketing to be effective, you need a profound understanding of your ideal clients - their age, gender, social status, their likes, dislikes, problems they face in organizing, channels they use for information, etc.

Construct a powerful website, one that effortlessly communicates the essence of your brand, showcases your services and achievements, and has a smooth user interface. Include testimonials from satisfied clients and offer useful content like blogs or infographics to increase your site's visibility and credibility.

Harness the power of social media. Create engaging content across platforms like Facebook, Instagram, and LinkedIn to interact with your potential clients. Visual documentation of before-and-after organizing projects can capture users' attention and gain potential clients.

Email marketing is another cost-effective tool. By sending personalized and informative e-mails to your potential clients, you can nurture your leads and turn them into your customers.

10.3. Increasing Revenue with Service Diversification

While your core service is organizing, you can amplify your revenue by offering complementary services. These could include decluttering consultation, organizing workshops, virtual organizing, or selling organizing products like labels or storage bins, allowing you to tap into different revenue streams.

Consider package-based pricing. This allows customers to choose based on their needs and feels more personalized. It also provides pre-set choices, which breaks down the services and costs in a more digestible way for your clients.

10.4. Fostering Strategic Partnerships

Partnering with businesses that complement your services can provide access to a larger client base. For instance, pairing with interior designers, property managers, or event planners will give you an opportunity to showcase your skills to their clientele.

It's essential to choose your partnerships wisely and ensure the association aligns with your business values. The objective is to create a win-win situation for both parties that leads to mutual growth.

10.5. Investing in Learning and Development

To keep pace with the rapidly growing demand and competition, continuous learning and development is crucial. Attend workshops, events, and conferences related to organizing and entrepreneurship. These platforms cater to opportunities to learn from industry leaders, meet potential clients, and network with peers.

You can further bolster your credibility by earning certifications from recognized institutions. This adds an edge of professionalism to your business and instills confidence in your clients about your expertise.

10.6. Building a High-performing Team

As your business grows, it becomes increasingly challenging to manage all clients single-handedly. Hiring and developing a high-performing team of professional organizers is necessary to handle the growing workload.

Identify the skills you need for your team, draft roles and responsibilities, and invest time in team training. Nurture a workplace culture where ideas are shared, and achievements are recognized, leading to increased productivity and employee satisfaction.

Remember that growth is a journey, not a destination, and every successful journey requires careful planning, persistence, and agility to adapt to the change. Scaling a professional organizing business fits into this mold of growth. In this trajectory of expansion, let the purpose of helping others find peace and productivity in their spaces be your driving force.

Chapter 11. Case Studies: Success Stories and Lessons Learned

Organizing homes and businesses, crafting serene spaces out of chaos, can be an overwhelming task to startup, especially navigating the entrepreneurial labyrinth. No two journeys are the same. However, understanding the path traveled by successful predecessors can yield valuable insights for your own venture. The following case studies unearth the trials, tribulations, and triumphs of successful professional organizers — the Home Organizing Gurus. Their stories shed light on valuable lessons and the keys to success in this field.

11.1. The Serene Space: Annabelle's Beautiful Organizing Venture

Annabelle, a stay-at-home mom, used the free time gifted to her when her children began school to turn her passion for organization into a thriving business. Starting with a DIY website and creating a strong social media presence, she leveraged her day-to-day organizing methods as content. She began by showcasing her own home's transformation and later that of her friends, which catapulted her venture.

Succinct Key Takeaways and Lessons Learned: * Utilize social media platforms to reach out and showcase your work effectively. * Start with organizing familiar spaces and use the experience to explore further. * Authenticity connects with the audience on a more profound level.

11.2. The Tidied Mart: Elizabeth's Retail Store Transformation Saga

Elizabeth, a former retail store manager, used her industry experience to launch a successful professional organizing business. She spotted a unique opportunity in assisting retail stores struggling with clutter and poor spatial organization. Her approach involved not just construction of serene spaces, but also implementing systems to sustain the same.

Succinct Key Takeaways and Lessons Learned: * Leveraging industry-specific skills can set you apart from the competition. * An effective organizing system will yield long-term benefits and secure repeat clientele. * Target niche markets to distinguish your services.

11.3. The Corporate Organizer: Mike's Transition From Chaos to Clarity

Mike, a former corporate executive, used his understanding of the corporate world to create a successful professional organizing business. Mike offered specialized services catering to corporates, assisting them with paper management, digital file organization, office space decluttering and time management consultations.

Succinct Key Takeaways and Lessons Learned: * Diversify your offerings based on the needs of your clients. * Integration of physical and digital organizational systems is key in the contemporary business environment. * Optimizing clients' productivity through time management is a value-addition many businesses appreciate.

11.4. The Passionate Minimalist: Sarah's Leap From Passion to Profit

Sarah, a self-proclaimed minimalist, used her passion for simplicity and decluttering to establish a distinctive organizing business. She catered to clients looking for a lifestyle change and desired a move towards minimalism. Sarah's services expanded, offering decluttering, systematic organization, and ongoing support for a minimalist lifestyle.

Succinct Key Takeaways and Lessons Learned: * Use your specific passion within the organization field to niche down services. * Sustainable organization is about changing habits, not only decluttering. Offer comprehensive services. * Client support is crucial for maintaining a decluttered and organized lifestyle.

Each of these successful entrepreneurs experienced different challenges and victories, but all have made a mark through their distinctive services. As you navigate your path to becoming a Home Organizing Guru, bear these lessons in mind, cultivate your unique approach, and brace yourself for the gratifying journey of turning mess into order while creating a thriving business.

www.ingramcontent.com/pod-product-compliance
Lightning Source LLC
Chambersburg PA
CBHW072217290526
45794CB00007B/2785